My Fur Is Thick and Spotted

by Jessica Rudolph

Consultants:
Christopher Kuhar, PhD
Executive Director
Cleveland Metroparks Zoo
Cleveland, Ohio

Kimberly Brenneman, PhD
National Institute for Early Education Research
Rutgers University
New Brunswick, New Jersey

BEARPORT
PUBLISHING

New York, New York

Credits

Cover, © Ian Rentoul/Shutterstock; 4–5, © iStockphoto/Thinkstock; 6–7, © Stefan Bader; 8–9, © Tom Soucek/Alaska Stock/Corbis; 10–11, © Animal Imagery/Alamy; 12–13, © Ian Rentoul/Shutterstock; 14–15, © olga_gl/Shutterstock; 16–17, © Animal Imagery/Alamy; 18–19, © age fotostock/Alamy; 20–21, © age fotostock/Alamy; 22, © Associated Press; 23, © iStockphoto/Thinkstock; 24, © Dennis Donohue/Shutterstock.

Publisher: Kenn Goin
Creative Director: Spencer Brinker
Design: Debrah Kaiser
Photo Researcher: Michael Win

Library of Congress Cataloging-in-Publication Data

Rudolph, Jessica.
  My fur is thick and spotted / by Jessica Rudolph.
     pages cm. — (Zoo clues)
  Includes bibliographical references and index.
  Audience: Ages 5–8.
  ISBN-13: 978-1-62724-113-7 (library binding)
  ISBN-10: 1-62724-113-2 (library binding)
  1. Snow leopard—Juvenile literature. I. Title.
  QL737.C23R83 2014
  599.75'55—dc23

                          2013036949

For more information, write to Bearport Publishing Company, Inc., 45 West 21st Street, Suite 3B, New York, New York 10010. Printed in the United States of America.

10 9 8 7 6 5 4 3 2 1

Contents

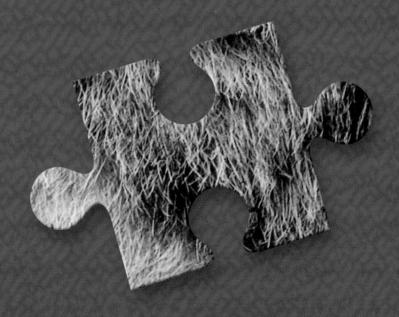

What Am I?

Look at my
whiskers.

4

They are long.

5

My paws
are big.

They have
sharp claws.

7

My ears are
short and round.

8

I have a fuzzy nose.

The tip is pink.

I have a long,
thick tail.

13

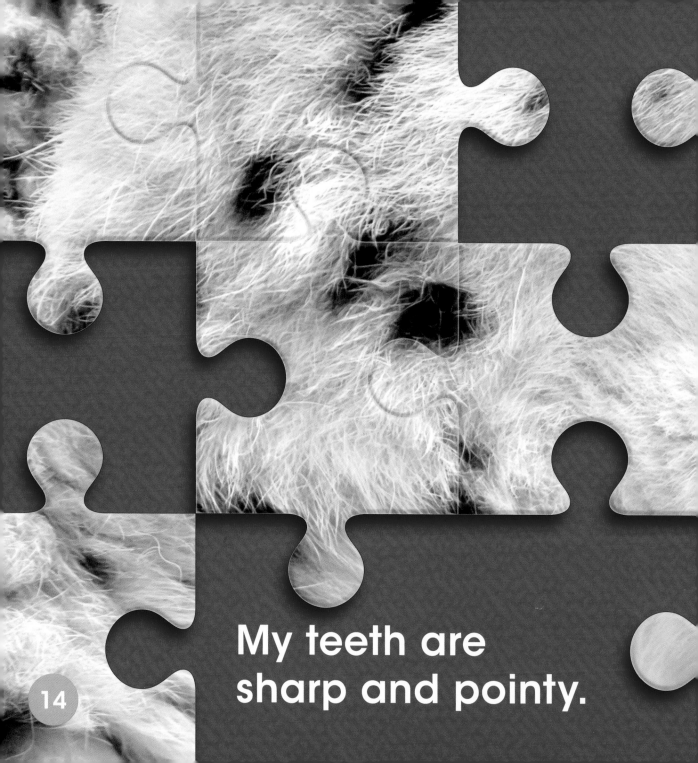

My teeth are
sharp and pointy.

14

My fur is soft
and thick.

16

It has black
spots.

What am I?

18

Let's find out!

19

I am a snow leopard!

21

Animal Facts

Snow leopards are mammals. Like almost all mammals, they give birth to live young. The babies drink milk from their mothers. Mammals also have hair or fur on their skin.

More Snow Leopard Facts

Food:	Sheep, goats, hares, birds, and deer
Size:	Up to 8 feet (2.4 m) long, including the tail
Weight:	Up to 120 pounds (54.4 kg)
Life Span:	Up to 13 years in the wild
Cool Fact:	Snow leopards use their fluffy tails like a blanket to cover themselves up in snowy weather.

Adult Snow
Leopard Size

Where Do I Live?

Snow leopards live in the cold, snowy mountains of Central Asia.

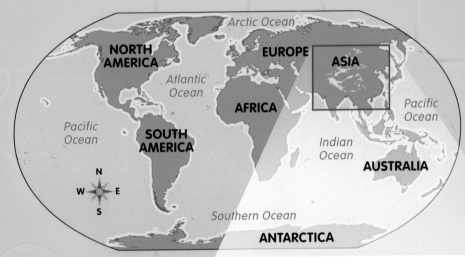

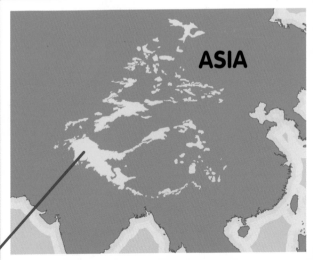

ASIA

Where snow
leopards live

Index

Read More

Poppenhäger, Nicole, Ivan Gantschev, and J. Alison James. *Snow Leopards.* New York: NorthSouth Books (2006).

Shores, Erika L. *Snow Leopards (Pebble Plus: Wildcats).* Mankato, MN: Capstone (2011).

Learn More Online

To learn more about snow leopards, visit
www.bearportpublishing.com/ZooClues

About the Author

Jessica Rudolph lives in Connecticut. She has edited and written many books about history, science, and nature for children.